CW00568659

To Alison,

A most creative soul...

Andrew

Machon   Feb 2008

A DIFFERENCE OF ONE

rediscovering a loving and creative originality

ANDREW MACHON

ACKNOWLEDGEMENTS

I am indebted to Gwil Roberts for his continual support, enthusiasm and guidance throughout the journey of composing this book. Special thanks are due to Thomas Moore, who not only contributed the preface, but gave such valuable advice and encouragement. I am indebted to Raffaella Barker for her appreciative and thoughtful words. I would also like to thank Piers Worth for fruitful discussions and the development of ideas. My thanks go also to Julie Schofield, Val Tomlin, Ed Young, Graham Peacock, Jill Jesson, Kathy Spitz, Edryd Sharp and Mary Ann Ephgrave. Sincere thanks also to Roger Maile for his rare combined talents employed in the design and editing of the book from its conception to completion. Finally, thanks to all those other friends, too numerous to detail individually, who have made valuable contributions and offered their support.

A DIFFERENCE OF ONE
rediscovering a loving and creative originality

Oliver's Books

Published in the UK by Oliver's Books
www.adifferenceofone.com
© Andrew Machon, 2008
The images and text in this book are the copyright of Andrew Machon who asserts his moral rights to be identified as the author of the work. Copyright, 2008.

British Library Cataloguing-in-Publication Data:
A catalogue record for the book is available from the British Library.

ISBN 978-0-9558185-0-9
First edition, 2008

Design and editorial production by Roger Maile Consultancy
20 St Peters Road, Croydon, CR0 1HD
Printed in England by Gemini Press Ltd.

All rights reserved. No part of this publication may be reproduced, transmitted in any form or by any means, or stored in a retrieval system of any nature, without the prior written permission of the publisher.

PREFACE
Thomas Moore

I have long been inspired by an image from Robert Fludd's book on the art of memory, which shows a man with a prominent bald skull and a large third eye labelled *oculus imaginationis*, the eye of imagination. Everything depends on how we imagine our world and ourselves. As we imagine, so we live and so we find our meaning.

Andrew Machon has a strong imaginal eye that looks at the world in a fresh and probing way. It is his images, so magnetic and stirring, so simple and yet so fresh, that draw me to his work. They show us what the world is and at the same time change it, giving it a new imaginal texture. We need this fresh imagination so that we don't live in a stale universe of meaning. Life moves along, and our imagination has to keep pace.

There are inspiring images of nature in this book, but also chairs and mannequins and ruins. Both nature and culture have a secret depth that can only be revealed by art and contemplation. Both natural objects and manufactured things have a soul, a mysterious depth that contains a secret vitality that we all need in order to be persons and personalities, subjects rather than objects.

Andrew would like to change this world so that its depth might allow for peace and conviviality. I think he appreciates the role of imagination in realising this goal. If we could picture a world that doesn't deal with conflict by resorting to violence, we might find alternatives. If we could imagine a world where competition would be friendly, not so absolute and literal, we might discover the joys of community.

A long tradition holds that art has powers of healing. If that is true, then this book should contribute to the healing of our troubled society. But how would this work, specifically and concretely? Readers could take time to contemplate the images and let the originality of the photographs make a slight change in vision. The artifice in the images, the fact that they have been 'doctored' and processed, gives them the power to propose a new world. They may take you further into experience than you have ventured before, and that inward advance may be healing.

People are often disturbed by an artistic image precisely because the image has the power to challenge a sense of meaning and stir emotions. But as the observer, you have to open yourself in reflection and wonder. You have to meditate on the image, let it sink in and do its work. If you want to be healed, you have to allow some change in how you see the world and your part in it.

I think I could contemplate the picture of the chair, the tree, and the landscape for many years. There is so much to consider, so much to look at, so many things to feel. This image could make you more sensitive and render your world less coarse and blunt. It could help you reconcile one of the most difficult confrontations of all: nature and culture.

The world is in a highly disturbed state today, violence everywhere indicating profound emotional and intellectual unsettling. It is also a world where contemplation and art are marginal, interesting perhaps but not at the centre of concern. A fresh artistic vision is not only valuable but necessary. We need to calm the savage breast and open our hearts and minds. Both goals could be accomplished through art, like Andrew's, that gives us a new way of seeing.

Thomas Moore,
Author of Care of the Soul *and many other books.*

Introduction

We have become tired and less forgiving of figures in authority who seek to charm us with their 'spin' rather than represent us from conviction and with authenticity. 'They' take critical decisions which may go against the core of our humanity, leaving us feeling deeply disillusioned and disempowered. We become alienated from the issues: they belong not to us, but to someone else – someone 'out there'.

It was this realisation that prompted me to start composing this work. I realised that I have repeatedly turned a blind eye to the most crucial dilemmas of our modern times, such as war and peace, disease and the destruction of our environment. It was not that I didn't care passionately about such matters on a personal level, but the feeling that these are issues beyond me, belonging to 'them'. This blind belief absolved me from any feeling of direct responsibility.

This book invites the reader to share in my personal journey of considering how we may move from blind reaction to be able to offer a more reflective and conscious response – to consider the part we may each play in making a difference of, and as, one.

Consider for a moment how different might we, others, our communities and the natural world be if we could see the impact of our blind reactions and instead be able to offer a more insightful response.

INTRODUCTION

We scratch only the surface.

Might we consider if such profound dilemmas have a common 'root' and originate from the very core of each of us? As we journey to realise our original nature, instead of turning away, are we being invited to learn how to be able to offer a more reflective response? Might the meaning and even resolution of such vital dilemmas paradoxically wait to be discovered from within, rather than be seen only as another's problem 'out there'?

Composing this book began with a conscious personal decision to turn to face these vital dilemmas and to contemplate my part in them. Of all the books I have, at various times, considered writing, this is the one I would wish to have completed if my life were suddenly to be ended. I do not pretend to offer 'the answer', but – through exploring the key questions – to foster new insight and to stimulate discussion and choice. I hope my personal journey, expressed in words and images, will help guide others to find their own response to a vital call that sounds from within our silence.

I dedicate this book to each and every person who has felt helpless in the face of such vital dilemmas as war and peace, living and dying and health and disease and who are losing heart in the belief that we cannot offer a meaningful response.

Time and again I am drawn to photograph the empty chair.
It is not a lonely place, but more an invitation
to remember a forgotten intimate relationship.

The Seasons
of the Self

In my work as a psychotherapist and life coach, I have realised time and again that one of the deepest motivations of the human being is to become a storyteller. We long to meet with 'the other' to whom we can open to tell. In meeting, we live out our inside story through whatever medium of expression we choose, be it word, music, song, image or dance.

If this longing is unfulfilled or even denied, we are destined to act out our story upon the world's stage as puppets. If we act unconsciously, when challenged we react. This 'play' ends only when we can open our eyes to see the person behind the actors' masks. Our challenge is therefore to awaken to recognise the actor, his many masks and indeed the play in which we have taken a starring role. We are free only when we can step from this 'stage' and can choose acting to be our profession or not.

This section of the book describes the journey of how we can more consciously live and tell our inside story. I refer to this as the 'seasons of the self', with four key phases: sleeping, awakening, becoming and returning.

Time and again, we are called to journey through the seasons of the self. For self is less an absolute, with a beginning or end, and more a continual iteration and new discovery. In the ever-changing seasons of self, might we learn to discern that which is changeless? Through making this journey, we open the door to discover our deeper, emerging self. This discovery empowers our ability to make the difference of one.

In the second part of the book, I explore how my own journey has illuminated some of the dilemmas that had previously appeared to be beyond, and outside of, me.

Are we a 'sleeping beauty', blind to the fact
that we await a special 'kiss' to awaken?

Sleeping

Like every other seed in nature, our seed-self is dormant
– sleeping without full awareness of its own potential and
possibility. Seasonally, this is the winter of the self. We may
be carried by external forces in the same way that a seed is
carried by the wind, a river or a bird, until we come to rest
upon a more fertile loam where we can at last awaken
and germinate.

As we sleep, so our eyes are closed to the world. It can be hard
to believe that even though we see outwardly with apparent
clarity and precision, we are in fact only partially sighted and
sleeping. As we discover ourselves, so we rediscover the world
around us. The lens of the self is not fixed or finite: our vision
will change to the same degree that we are able to open our
eyes to discover our original nature.

True vision is less dependent on what we see outwardly and
more on the degree to which we discover insight. Might we
then consider life to be a journey of learning how to see truly?
If so, one of the greatest challenges is how we can awaken to
realise that we are only partially sighted.

Before awakening more fully, do we sleepwalk through
days and nights, living within a dream-world? Are we a
'sleeping beauty', blind to the fact that we await a special
'kiss' to awaken?

Is our only certainty that we are a mystery?

We seem to live our lives largely through our heads and rational thinking. The eyes of rational thought largely see only problems to be analysed and solved. Instinctively, we perceive the search for the truth as the need to find something: most often, the 'right' answer. Though we pride ourselves in the certainty of our answers, could our need for surety be driven by the fear of the mystery of our original nature?

Might our only certainty be that we are a mystery and a continual discovery unto ourselves? If so, how may we open our eyes more fully to appreciate the mystery of self, rather than pushing this from the light of our awareness into the shadow?

Mystery exists beyond rational comprehension and yet it defines our being and may even be the source of our becoming. We are less fact and more possibility than we might at first believe.

How different might it be if we welcomed the expression of our creative mystery rather than fearing the irrational? What is the potential if, through our relationships, organisations and wider society, we embrace the unknown as that which longs to be known?

Have we blindly turned ourselves inside out?

We may see life as a journey to find the answer and to discover the one thing or something more that will finally complete and satisfy. This one thing may be, for example, more possessions, a better job or a perfect partner.

However, what if we have blindly turned our backs on a vital inner relationship and are seeking to find the 'something more' in the wrong place? In denying and fearing the mystery of the self, we appear to close our eyes to this dilemma and instead turn ourselves inside out. Our goal is then to find and make a trophy of the something more outside ourselves, rather than accepting the call of our inner journey and motivation to become the 'something more'.

In our blindness, do we turn away from that within, which we are then destined to seek outwardly? Blind to the futility of this search, we become a stranger to original self.

To observe ourselves, ever outwardly seeking the something more, we may be forgiven for thinking that we are becoming a race of 'human doings' who have forgotten our deeper inner nature as human beings. Do we fill our lives with activity only to find the secret of fulfilment is how to become empty?

Have we turned our backs on a vital inner relationship,
seeking to find the 'something more' in the wrong place?

Do we become blind to our blindness?

Our need to know may be no more than a front which hides our fear of uncertainty and the mystery of who we truly are. Might this obsession to know with certainty blind us to that which longs to be known?

This outward reaction and drive to find the answer that would complete and satisfy us can become habitual or even addictive. What then becomes the goal is the 'fix' that we get from the incessant search. As our searching becomes a major and routine part of our life, so we begin, in time, to close our eyes upon our partial sightedness and superficiality. We become blind to our blindness.

Being blind to our blindness, talk of 'awakening' is both irrational and impossible: a mystery that is likely to be strongly and firmly dismissed. To those who see through this, awakening presents vast potential and possibility. Our viewpoints are, therefore, dependent upon the stage of our own inner journey and can literally be a world apart.

We might sleepwalk across the entire globe for all our lives searching for the 'answer' without ever awakening to ask our vital 'questions'. Life may become an endless search along a blind alley. In this darkness, our actions are largely surface reactions – devoid of insight and conscious choice. They reflect the absence of our undiscovered original nature.

Like the blind who lead the blind, if we see only from within the rigid walls of our thinking, we may never open our eyes upon our deeper paradox and mystery. The limited confines of our thinking can trap and imprison the very freedom for which we long and search. We may live life only from our heads, ever blind to the closeness of the heart – less than one breath away.

Must we first lose the key in order to find the lock?

Is true sight born of seeing blindness?

Have you ever wondered if at some point in our journey we have known a moment of perfect vision? If so, does this memory remain as a life long aspiration, inner motivation, beacon and guide? Is this an inner flame that flickers but never fails? Might we be able to see our blindness and limitation in the light of this memory?

It is only when we can surrender our certainty and, for a moment, step out of ourselves that we remember and can open our eyes to see who we may be. From knowing of our limitation, might we discover new insight?

If we surrender the need to be perfect, we can awaken to our limitations and vulnerability. Paradoxically, in meeting with our imperfection, might we then be able to open our eyes to see beyond and glimpse that which is perfect and without limitation?

Like the blind who lead the blind,
if we see only from within the rigid walls of our thinking,
we may never open our eyes upon our deeper paradox and mystery.

Is surrender the art and practice of self care?

Those who stretch outwardly for perfection set impossible expectations for themselves and others. In reaching for the impossible, the perfectionist can blindly and cruelly deny any self knowledge of imperfection and vulnerability. Perfection may not be a 'prize' we can claim directly. However, if we can surrender the need to have, then perfection may ever motivate and inspire our becoming. Paradoxically, as we embrace the lesser and limited, can we open our eyes to the 'more than' and that which is without limitation?

As we surrender our need to be perfect, we can open our eyes to see the cruel expectations we have placed on ourselves and others. In the act of surrender, we are given another chance to embrace, with new affection, those limited and vulnerable aspects of ourselves that we have judged to be bad and blindly banished to our shadow. This remembering fosters forgiveness and compassion and can offer a growing sense of integrity, identity and self-esteem. In accepting our fragility, we discover our inner strength.

In being willing to meet with our own limitations are we, in turn, met by love and compassion? In the moment of surrender, we may open to a vital gift of unconditional care.

We search ever outwardly for love. Paradoxically might love wait patiently for us just beyond the visible and our need to find? The need to search, to know and to find feeds only more neediness. There is no wisdom in continuing to feed an insatiable appetite. Instead, might we learn how to soothe that which hungers?

Do we seek the innocent and fresh eyes of the child?

Awakening

Paradoxically, the self must first become still before it can quicken. We awaken in the same moment that we can open our eyes to see our blindness.

Who or what awakens us from the darkness and dormancy of winter to experience the springtime of the self? Do we seek the innocent and fresh eyes of the child? Or can we borrow the unconditional eyes of an 'inner optician' that can observe and reveal our blindness to us?

Remember the story of the child who once looked upon the emperor and confidently observed what adult eyes would not see, that he was in truth wearing no clothes. Like the emperor, do we remain unaware of our naked superficiality? And yet, do we also long to be seen and discovered through new eyes?

By nature's stillness
I am most profoundly moved.

Can nature mirror our own original nature?

In developing this book, I have been repeatedly drawn to natural settings. These were my quiet lay-bys beside the busy road of routine living. Here I could at last contemplate.

Maybe nature presents a vast otherness which draws us to be still, offering ample space to pause and reflect.

Can we accept this open-ended invitation to look beyond our current situation and awaken to share in a new outlook and vision?

As we look to nature, we remember our natural rhythm and recollect our inner story.

En pointe

There are rare moments, just as the day awakens, when nature appears to stand still. It is as if nature knows a secret to which we may awaken and upon which we can but gaze and wonder. This is not anticipation, but more a complete satisfaction.

If only I could give voice or verse to such stillness. It is as if nature, the ballerina, stands en pointe, perfectly poised. And we, the audience, can only gasp at her artistry and confidence.

When all movement ends, might we then glimpse that which animates? I am certain only of the mystery and profound beauty before my eyes which take away my breath, as I too, pause.

In this moment, the pendulum of nature's clock is stilled to a final 'tick'. And in a long exhalation, time comes to rest quietly and silently on every mountain crest and sylph-like cloud. Time stops. To relax with the eternal.

Eventually, persuaded by the touch of the breeze, nature breathes back in. And so resounds a 'tock'.

And a key turns in my lock.

Nature's inspiration

Nature seems to share our conscience in reminding us of that which we so often forget. As we reflect upon the beauty of this vast otherness, do we recall an other that we have forgotten – a vital memory of original self?

In sharing in the mystery of the landscape, we can recall a memory of our own mysterious uncharted inner landscapes. Maybe nature invites us to remember the stranger within.

Might a part of the gift be the larger perspective that nature can offer our insularity, with the promise of a fresh outlook?

Our arrogance is dwarfed by nature's wonder.

Natural remedy

Have we lost sight of our relationship with nature to the same degree that we are blind to our original nature?

Is nature today somehow out of kilter and the distinct identity of her seasons more confused? Our identity may be more closely aligned with nature's than we might imagine. If the natural world presents us with a mirror of the gap between our superficiality and aspiration for a deeper identity, there may be no need other than to look all around us to see our illustrated story.

Might the realisation of our true relationship with nature therefore provide a natural remedy and solution? As we open to discover our deeper nature and identity, might we in this process innately help nature to retune and realign to hers?

The solution we seek may not be a single answer but more the composite and emerging result of how we answer and respond to a vital calling. How different might we, others and our natural world become if we were to realise our original nature? As we respond to the unveiling of our deeper nature, this natural remedy may emerge into society.

Nature's invitation

Might nature help us remember and rediscover a lost intimacy?

The challenge is to accept the invitation to discover nature more subjectively rather than to judge only with objective certainty. Might our resolution be a little less rational and a little more relational than we might at first have thought?

This may turn our thinking inside out. Certainly our relationship with nature now becomes less the problem and more the possible solution. Can we therefore begin to see nature more as our guide and vital teacher?

We may have forgotten that we are an innate part of this natural line and shared ancestry. Nature is not a mere acquaintance and an object for analysis, but more family and our next of kin. How different might it be if we cared for the natural world as if it were our most beloved family?

Time and again I am drawn to photograph the empty chair in nature. It is not a lonely place to which I am drawn, but more a reminder and invitation to remember an intimate and vital relationship.

Just beyond the visible is there an ever present otherness which patiently awaits our acquaintance and calls us inward to sit and reflect?

Maybe our challenge is how to give shape and form to such mystery without making it false with too much fact?

Through nature's otherness can we remember and recall the relationship with our own 'inner other'? Is this the 'inner optician' that can reveal, assess and amend our partial sightedness?

Maybe in truth it is the inner other that offers an empty chair where we can rest and reflect within. From this chair, can we share in the vision of new and fresh eyes through which we can look in upon ourselves with true clarity and precision and see our blindness? Perhaps we may then look out upon the world with new insight.

Might the attraction to the empty chair found in nature be a vital, yet forgotten, memory of the 'chair within' – a place and point from which we can witness our original nature?

Might it be our natural destiny to meet with the mystery and paradox of the self – that is, if we can stop the incessant search to find it? Our lifelong search to find our most 'significant other' may end only when we see the wisdom in looking just beyond the need to search.

*Might nature help us remember
and rediscover a lost intimacy?*

*Maybe in truth it is the inner other that offers an empty chair
where we can rest and reflect within.*

Just beyond the visible is there an ever-present otherness
which patiently awaits our acquaintance
and calls us inward to sit and reflect?

Is there a self-fulfilling prophecy?

As a moth to a strange light, are we each attracted to remember and realise our original nature?

When we awaken to take our place on the inner empty chair, we automatically invite others to share in this experience. There are moments when, in the presence of that one special person, we can suddenly open to share and tell our inside story. What is sensed in that moment is a quality of unconditional attention, compassion and love.

Is this a self-fulfilling prophecy? As we discover our original nature, do we openly hold and offer this possibility for all others? As we see and learn how to surrender our many masks, we may humbly offer others the same chance.

Puppet or puppeteer?

As we awaken to truly see ourselves, others and the world around us through the untainted and unconditional eyes of this inner other, we discover the relationship between puppet and puppeteer.

Paradoxically, we act like puppets only when we lose sight of the guiding hand of the other within. If we are blind to the inner other, we become self-absorbed and reactive; we harden and live superficially. Flesh becomes wood.

Wood becomes flesh only when our eyes are opened to see beyond the confines of the self that sleeps. We awaken when we remember the dynamic paradox of our deeper nature. This is the vital impulse that motivates our becoming.

In dying, do we find the secret of how to live?

The moment we start to unveil our blindness and discover the emerging self, we can surrender our delusions of omnipotence. We are invited instead to embrace lovingly our imperfection and vulnerability.

Do we, therefore, awaken to our limitation together with the realisation that we are dying? Death is the great unknown. It can fill the rational mind with fear and drive its search for surety. We may blindly react to this fear by banishing death from our lives.

However, what if dying holds the only key which can unlock life?

That we emerge is a revelation.

Becoming

What we awaken to is the invitation to participate in the creative mystery of becoming. This realisation of our deeper nature may give profound direction to our lives and an experience of 'breakthrough'. So we move into the summertime of the self, and can see our potential for growth: where the acorn awakens to the vision of the oak that it longs and intends to become.

Change emerges naturally as we remember that which is vital and marry our intentions with our inspiration. Together these are the dual flames of the beacon that ever lights and guides our becoming. So we shape our thoughts and longings into new realities, extending our vision to the horizon of our imagination. Through our imagination, we can conceive in reality that which we perceive as possibility.

In reacting, are we blind to a vital motivation?

In awakening to the place of the inner other, we become a witness both to ourselves and to others. Here we may ever orientate, rest and balance through the discovery of an inner compass.

Through the eyes of this inner observer, we can see both our potential and partial sightedness. In these moments we may be gifted with insight and foresight. From this new inner viewpoint, we realise that the endless outward drive to search is an innate motivation to become that 'something more'.

That which we are driven to search for is what we are called to discover within and to become.

If we remain blind to this inner source of our innate desire and motivation, we may reject the very thing for which we are then destined to search outwardly – maybe for the rest of our lives. That is, until the moment when we learn how to see beyond the need to search. Then, and only then, do we return home.

As our rational head remembers the spacious invitation of our heart to experience and feel, we can embrace and appreciate more fully the paradox and mystery of our original nature. Now our thinking can expand beyond the need to answer with swift finality and take more time to reflect upon the mystery and possibility of this deeper inner relationship.

Rather than being driven to answer, we are at last free to choose to contemplate and ask our most vital questions. Without urgency or the need to solve, we can allow the deeper meaning of our life and work to emerge.

Am I an island,
an undiscovered continent
and uncharted ocean?

A vital and vibrant dynamic
which may be the source
of our motivation and becoming.

Is the core of our nature a vital and creative paradox?

We each strive to be an individual – distinct from all others. Equally, however, we each long to find our place and belong as a part of something more, in the same way that a piece fits within a jigsaw. So we are at the same time singular, in seeking to separate and differentiate ourselves from others, and plural, in longing to integrate and find belonging in community and the loving embrace of others.

This apparently irreconcilable paradox is at the core of human nature. It is a vital and vibrant dynamic and may be the source of our motivation and becoming which ever seeks creative expression in our life and work.

Maybe we are best described as poets who seek to express their creative mystery in verse, rather than actors who, upon the stage of the world, read their lines with given predictability.

Ancient youth

My father said, "I am 90 years of age and yet something in me still feels twenty-one." We laughed with both joy and sadness.

Is there an ancient youth who ever seeks expression through each and all of us? Is this the source of our being that is ever vital, whom we forever aspire to be and become?

If you forget this ancient youth, then simply look to nature and there you will recall a memory.

Gaze upon the vastness of rock shaped into the majesty of mountains and something age old may stir in you. For there is a vital calling beyond all fossilisation. Sit beside the sea and be lulled by the melody of the youthful advance then ageing decline of your tide.

Let us come to know the youth who, irrespective of our years, longs to live life to the full; who awakens our deadened wood into new leaf and bud and is ever springtime and a longing in the heart's every winter.

This youth is ancient too – maybe millions of years. Is this a wise and benevolent being whose knowledge extends beyond our lives and may encompass all others – ever watching, ever guiding, ever knowing and ever loving?

Have you seen how such age old wisdom can shine through
the eyes of a child who somehow seems to know of everything
before the complication of words?

Can this wisdom be born in us again, I wonder?

As we age, how might we learn to see our blindness and so
surrender our many masks until we unveil once more the eyes
and innocence of the child?

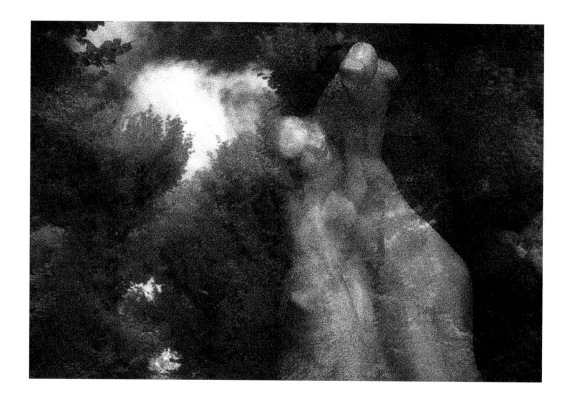

If you forget this ancient youth,
then simply look to nature
and there you will recall a memory.

Do we evolve in discovering the inner observer?

To know and experience the place of the inner witness is to embrace the creative mystery of self. The eyes of the inner observer can see the paradox of our nature without fear or judgement.

Might there be a gradual emergence and maturing of this inner witness, which becomes fine-tuned through repeated reference and inner conversation? Let me, for now, describe this evolving awareness of the observer as the emergence of our deeper conscience. You may prefer to choose another name: in essence, what we wish to name is our emerging original self – the inner reference which seeks expression in everything we say, how we see and what we choose to do.

Conscience holds the memory of that which is most original in us and with this the promise we long to fulfil. Through this inner dialogue, we are kept honest to ourselves and are guided in how to become the person we aspire to be.

Echoes of past judgemental voices, such as those of parents and teachers, direct us in what we should do. They represent the thwarted expectations of key figures in our past life and not necessarily our own. The volume and intensity of these voices reduce as that of our conscience emerges and becomes clearer and more singular. We grow to feel greater comfort and security with ourselves, realising that we feel – and are – good enough.

As we remember and meet with our limitations and vulnerabilities, we can invite back the aspects of our self that we have mislabelled as 'bad' and once wished to banish. In such moments of returning, we can open to the experience of forgiveness and begin to unload the burden of guilt forged by others' directive voices. It is part of our journey of becoming not only to resolve our feelings of guilt, but to forgive those who fostered them. The voice of our emerging conscience is compassionate, kind and forgiving. We can forgive others only to the same degree that we can firstly forgive ourselves.

As we journey to realise our original nature and deeper self, a singular inner presence emerges and remains.

This ever present inner reference guides our actions and offers us untainted vision so that we may come to see goodness, love and wisdom. With the emergence of conscience comes the potential for a new way of relating to ourselves, others and our natural world.

This inner 'voice' is wise beyond my own years. I believe this may speak from a vast collective wisdom to illuminate a receptive mind.

It is an inner compass that can measure and remind us of the distance that we may stray from that which is vital, whilst ever offering to re-orientate and guide us back home.

My emerging conscience is a loving companion and inseparable guide. In this continual discovering, my eyes are opened to who I truly am.

We search all our lives for a mentor and yet overlook the one within. What if our most significant other, for whom we have endlessly searched, waits all of our lives to meet with us and welcome us home?

With the discovery of another within,
the boundaries of inner and outer dissolve.

Can we discover a multi-dimensional vision and thinking?

The wisdom of original self seems to extend beyond me and may encompass all others. Might we therefore each become open to receive and express a collective wisdom?

The boundaries of inner and outer seem to dissolve with the discovery of another within. Our senses open to both an individual and a collective experience. Through the emergence of the place of the inner observer – or 'I' – do we open an inner eye which can see both the 'it' and the 'we'?

As we discover the paradox and mystery of self, we are invited to accommodate a more multi-dimensional perspective and expand our vision and ability to sense. The many facets of the gem-like self emerge into our awareness.

As we journey to discover our original nature, our vision is both changed and shaped by this experience. We can open to receive not only the gift of insight but also intuition and, sometimes, rare moments of illumination.

In expanding our vision we equally extend our ability to think and sense. The drive and urgency to answer begins to balance with the newly found ability to relate and embrace more deeply. Here once more, the head remembers the heart and invites a more soulful, natural and authentic response. Our drive to answer may blindly steal away the only chance to contemplate and respond to our most vital questions and dilemmas.

It is important to realise that, despite our need to find them, our answers might be like gates that in our certainty we blindly and firmly close before us, barring further vital steps towards the discovery of original self. In the finality of believing that we know the answer, we may prematurely end that which ever longs to begin – and with it our ambition to become all that we may be.

As we surrender what is known, we remember that which longs to be known and which can illuminate our life from the depth of our shadow and the edge of our consciousness. Within the shadow and mystery of who we are, might we find the missing pieces to our vital jigsaw for which we have searched endlessly? Paradoxically, the parts of us which we disown and have sought to banish may, in truth, complete our integrity.

It is only when our mind and heart can join to embrace paradox, which our rational thinking fears as mystery, that we can free ourselves to become all that we may be. Might this be a clue to the meaning of life's journey?

We can value our answers whilst equally being willing to surrender them to recall a vital memory and longing beneath. Our answers become less a truth and end in themselves and more the platform from which we take a further step to consider the questions that are most vital to ourselves, each other and society.

Sit beside the sea and be lulled by the melody
of the youthful advance, then ageing decline, of your tide.

We arrive home only when we remember our original nature.

Returning

In the seasons of the self we reach autumn and the formation of the fruit of our journey together with a return to the seed and source. It is a season of both fruition and decay.

There are moments in life when we feel we have truly found and returned home. Though we seek to find, create or build the perfect home throughout our life, we arrive home only when we realise original self. As we realise our original nature, we find the comfort of home and a belonging in our own skin.

In these moments of becoming, we experience our most natural self. Happiness is the simplicity and contentment in accepting one's original nature.

Such an experience of homecoming, belonging and happiness can never be actively found – it is lost the very moment we try to find it. It is more the complete satisfaction of surrendering the need to find; for there, and only then, do we advance the discovery of original self.

If our thinking thirsts only for the answer, then we stray further from the welcome and quiet oasis of the heart. At home with our original nature, the heart and mind find their natural communion as we experience the mystery and paradox of soul. The quality and intimacy with which we relate to ourselves, others and nature profoundly deepen as we realise both the part and oneness of all.

The drive to find the 'something more' ends only when we realise that we aspire to be and become 'this'. Beyond the need to do, we can simply be ourselves.

Beyond the impulse to react, we find a deeper place from which we can respond. In the security of knowing one's original self and no longer needing to know, we are free to become all that we may long to be. Mystery is not only the unknown and what we fear, but might it also be the very essence of our humanity – the source and creative expression of that which longs to be known?

As we resist our neediness and relax our urgency, the qualities of compassion and love emerge into our lives. In resisting the temptation to find, we find our original nature.

In moments of completion, the beginning and ending of the journey dissolve to reveal only the simple wonder of having arrived. As we return home and remember our original nature, a presence replaces our pretence.

Wisdom cannot be taken or claimed, but is the gift to those who can surrender the need to find or have it.

We search all our lives to find love. Might it wait patiently for our return when our need to find is over? As a cloud forgives its form to sky, so we surrender and return to our source.

Beyond our every need, love, peace and wisdom are the 'original family' to which we return – a family that waits patiently to welcome us home. In opening to our original nature, are we being invited to learn how to care, love and act wisely?

As a cloud forgives its form to sky,
so we surrender and return to our source.

The Difference
of One

I started this book by referring to my feeling of impotence in
the face of the 'big issues' of the day – such as peace, disease
and environmental destruction.

In the first section, exploring the seasons of the self, I have
presented my belief that 'the answer' lies in surrendering the
need to find answers 'out there' and instead to look within.

Only by recognising our inner blindness can we commence
the process of opening our eyes to our original nature, its
mystery and paradox. By returning home to the emerging self,
we find the strength and insight to offer a more authentic and
loving response.

I did not want to leave this exploration without sharing how
my own inner journey is influencing my response to the issues
that I had previously felt to be beyond and outside me. My
selection of subjects and the views expressed are personal.
It is not intended as a blueprint to 'put the world to rights',
but an illustration of how we all have the potential to make a
difference of one.

If we see our emotions less as our closest friends and more as enemies,
we stray further from our original nature and that which is vital
to life and health.

Health and Disease

To learn to love without condition is a rare gift. As a psychotherapist, I realise time and again that it is not what I do, but more how I am, which fosters healing and growth. In our need to find a cure, have we become blind to that which truly heals? To be love is more than enough and requires no further action.

There are certain vital relationships which may be rare but, when found, can foster healing and growth. This quality of relationship is the inspired intention of the therapist, coach, mentor and sometimes a special loved one or best friend. In the presence of someone who is a trusting and loving witness are we given permission to open to tell our inside story?

As a society, we seem to be so concerned with finding a cure for disease that, in our relentless search, we can become blind to the power of relationship to heal. Paradoxically, our blind search for the answer or the cure can sever the very relationship that is vital to our health and well being. Might we consider if our healing depends as much on the quality of relationship with the physician as the remedies prescribed?

What qualities of relationship can heal? The qualities of love and compassion and the depth and focus of our attention may be the key. As we experience this gift of relationship, do we attune and remember a vital forgotten relationship? It is only through the eyes of the inner observer that we too can learn to see unconditionally with love and compassion in becoming a witness to ourselves and others.

Although we search for a cure, might there be a more natural remedy? Do we heal to the same extent that we can surrender and return into the loving embrace of self and the inner other? This may be a life's work – to be and become an unconditional witness of original self in service of others.

Health and healing is a vital inner orientation and conscious aspiration. In remembering that which is vital to our lives, can we constantly orientate, balance, revitalise and heal?

If we lose sight of that which is vital within, our anxiety and fears naturally build. In truth, these emotions are a measure of the degree to which we stray from our deeper and original self. If we are willing to meet with them, they serve as a natural barometer and guide.

The intimate invitation to relate with and simply experience our emotions presents the rational mind with more of a mystery and less of a solution. Our emotions are less objects to be analysed and more natural subjects to be experienced and lived. Therefore, in seeking to rationalise, the mind – even with all its intelligence – severs a vital relationship. Rationalisation can widen the perceived gap between the head and the heart, creating more feelings of detachment, depression and ultimately alienation.

How might we learn to educate our thinking to consider our emotions less as enemies and more as our closest allies, who seek only to guide us towards emerging self?

Our emotions wish only to keep us honest to ourselves. In fearing that which cannot be known and solved, our rational thinking fragments its self and then begins the lifetime search for the answer that will satisfy and complete.

The degree to which we can relate and know original self is the same degree to which we can relate with others. In denying our emotions, we may profoundly limit our capacity to relate. Our emotions wish only to help us remember who we are and invite a more intimate relationship with, and understanding of, self and thus others. Are we able to surrender our surety in order to cultivate a deeper emotional awareness, sensitivity and learning?

Our emotions hold the secret and memory of the natural bridge between the head and heart and can guide us back to this realisation and thus a chance to live more soulfully: that is, intimately in touch with both nature and our original nature.

The certainty of our answers and objectivity of our rational thinking imprison us in our heads. The heart, in contrast, longs only to experience subjectively the loving embrace without condition or end. For the heart, the embrace is an end in itself. In meeting with the mind, the unbridled passion of the heart can be tempered by reason. In the heart's embrace, the mind's thinking can at last relax its relentless searching and instead find ample space to reflect more upon the vital questions. With the heart, the mind can become informed by intuition and inspired choice to act. Collectively the mindful heart and heartfelt mind invite a more insightful response.

As we embody the paradox of our true nature, head and heart naturally reunite and we are no longer strangers to soul and our originality. The communion of head and heart opens our awareness to the creative discovery and expression of both 'what is' (our presence and being) and the aspiration, possibility and potential of 'what may be' (our becoming).

In fearing the mystery of the unknown and, indeed, our original nature, we deny and betray our emotions.

If we see our emotions less as our closest friends and more as enemies, we stray further from our original nature and that which is vital to life and health. In denying how we fear the mystery of who we are and in our unwillingness to relate, our anxiety and habitual activity increases and we can enter the state of dis-ease.

We may seek to push and banish our emotions to the edge of our awareness and beyond, yet they never fully disappear. If they did, they would take with them the only key which can unlock and free a more original way of being. However, as we seek to separate our emotions from us, we split ourselves from our power and potential. As we seek to imprison our emotions, we instead are imprisoned.

Our partial thinking is blind to our vital oneness. The magnitude of our emotions amplifies as we seek to deny and push them away. Like the fury and desperation of those who have been wrongly condemned, as we banish our emotions, we can unwittingly make monsters of them. At the edge of our awareness, instead of guiding our natural response, our discarded and devalued emotions may in moments of untimely and blind reaction suddenly steal from our shadow with harsh, critical and often desperate expression. When rejected, the once natural flow and invitation of emotions becomes a torrent and force beyond our control.

For in denying our fear, we give away our power to be governed beyond our control. In this way, our denied emotions make puppets of us all. Must we re-enact our untold story time and again until we meet the person who deems to know us beyond our wooden frame?

Though we banish them, our forgotten emotions still long to be remembered and call to us. Might we consider and imagine what value there may be in befriending rather then seeking to banish?

Continual denial may propel our emotions deeper into our shadow. This is the distant boundary to our conscious awareness. Here, our emotions exist in our outer space like lost satellites tracking a distant orbit, continuing to pulse back a signal and hoping one day that they will be remembered and deciphered.

Such continual denial only buries our emotions deeper within the bedrock of self, where they may begin to ossify like living fossils. Might such neglected and alienated aspects of our selves, when pushed beyond the edge of our awareness, become the very symptoms of our disease?

Might both the memory and content of key chapters of our untold story be locked away and encoded within our blind reactions and symptoms? But have we the capacity to remember and truly to listen and hear? Disease calls us to stop and contemplate the meaning of our lives, offering another chance to reorientate to that which is vital and healing.

As we seek to cure, we must not forget our symptoms and so silence the only voice which might naturally guide us towards a state of health and well-being. How can we resist the temptation and urgency to find the cure in order that we do not turn a blind eye to the co-ordinates within our symptoms which could orientate us towards health?

Through our symptoms, we may be guided back to remember aspects of our self that we have banished to the shadows and which long to be reborn into the light of our awareness. As we embrace these forgotten aspects of the self, we foster our sense of identity, integrity and completeness. Do we heal when we remember and experience our original nature: that which is complete and unbroken? In seeking to cure, we may become blind to the vital aspiration to be healthy.

And there in the stillness of complete surrender,
what might transform and who may emerge?

The journey towards our original nature is one of remembering those aspects of the self which we have feared and banished. These lost parts help build the jigsaw of the original self. In the alchemy of remembering, we deepen our awareness and find the choice to transform our reactions into a reflective, conscious response.

Surrender is the art and practice of courageously and consciously letting go of the known in order to remember and embrace more fully that which we have forgotten.

What of the ultimate surrender: that of all that we have and own as we approach our death? In dying, do we therefore heal? Or does death steal?

Maybe the answer we have searched for all our lives we discover through our conscious practice of the art of surrender in life. Each time we surrender, we experience a loss and a giving up – a little death. However, might this be only a part of the story? As we have explored, in surrendering we equally and quite paradoxically, invite the emergence of a little life. This is the chance for that which is vital and calls to be remembered to find expression and guide our becoming.

We need to become aware of that which is not yet known, whilst equally being able to let go of that which we have outgrown. Can we be more like the caterpillar who learns to shed and surrender many skins until it is time at last to enter the dark dormancy of our chrysalis? And there in the stillness of complete surrender, what might transform and who may emerge?

In surrendering,
we invite the emergence
of a little life.

Carry life
gently
as snow.

War and Peace

Do the drive for war and the aspiration for peace share a common root and source within each of us?

There can be no prospect of lasting peace as long as war is seen only as a problem 'out there' – on some other battlefield that we watch from the comfort of our armchair. Such safe viewing frankly denies that the responsibility for war and peace rests in our own hands.

Outwardly war appears complex: shrouded in politics, history, geography and religion. Can we look inwardly to see more clearly if war and peace might share a common origin within each of us? Might this dilemma be better understood from the inside out, rather than the outside in?

To expand our understanding of the nature of war and the quest for peace, we may first need to recognise our inner battlefield and the conflicts that we fight within. Consider the aspect or part of you which is ever needy and hungers for more, be it power, money, security or land. This part is demanding and would fight to secure these goals. Consider how, paradoxically, inner fragility may foster outward force – even brutality.

In our blindness, we do not see how the battle is lost the very moment it has begun. For how do you feed and satisfy that which ever hungers for something more?

If we could open our eyes to view this situation more fully, we might see that what we feel we need to take from others by force is already ours to claim – that is, if we can learn to see just beyond our need to take. How futile war is if the very thing we fight for is ever ours to claim from within. What we would fight for to our last breath may be ours to reclaim – less than one breath away.

Do we hunger for and wish to take from others that which we are blind to in ourselves?

Consider once more that aspect of your self which hungers for something more and the vital question of how we can feed the insatiable appetite. It can only be by soothing that which hungers. In this realisation we may find the true prospect for peace.

We cannot end the drive to fight through the brutality of another battle, but only through the gentle care and love for that part in each of us which ever hungers for something more.

We are driven to war, but truly do we hunger only for love? Is the power we crave outwardly driven by an absence of love within?

In essence, the option of peace may be embraced in a single choice: will we fight and kill repeatedly, or will we embrace with compassion and love? This choice is our's to take. And only we can make it.

If we learn how to soothe that which hungers within, might we then come to experience the inner power of having and being enough? In recognising our limitation and caring for our vulnerability, we can learn to see the 'more than' that we aspire to become. Through embracing our limitation and perceived weakness, we can harness our true power and strength. We can only forgive and love others if we can first learn to forgive and love ourselves.

As we forgive, we can put down our burdens of guilt, doubt and fear and realise our worth. With growing compassion and gentleness, we can soothe that which hungers. Maybe this is the only platform from which we can authentically make the choice for peace.

Only when we learn to see beyond the need to fight, can we see that the prize for which we have fought is already ours to claim. How can we learn to see our blindness? If we are blind to our blindness, then who is left to take responsibility for our reactions?

There is a hero in every one of us who one day learns when faced with another battle how to lay down the sword. In the wisdom of surrender and the choice not to fight, paradoxically we may claim that for which we have fought all our lives. Might peace possibly wait for us in abundance just beyond our every need?

What if the motivation and call to become more than we are has the same source as the drive to take more from others? The difference is that one is experienced as a reaction to take more and the other as a response and a vital aspiration to become the 'more than'. In our blindness, would we steal the very thing that in our wakefulness is ours to be realised?

Might the difference between going to war or choosing peace in our lives and the world be determined by our ability to listen, truly hear and respond, rather than react? If this is true, then we have forgotten and become blind to that which calls us to discover our deeper and original self.

Why do we fight for a cause, when our true cause is realised only when we can surrender the need to fight? Dare we imagine how the root of war in each of us might be a tragic and blind reaction to a misdirected call?

To choose peace, we must first awaken to distinguish between reaction and response. Then we may come to recognise that the source of our drive to take is also a vital motivation to become.

In this realisation, might we choose to lay down our weapons in remembering the aspiration and inner call to become all that we may be – both as individuals and collectively?

The choice for peace is a response we can consciously make beyond the need to react further. Consider how our behaviour may positively change towards ourselves, others, our communities and the natural world around us if we could offer a reflective response rather than blind reaction. How different might our impact, impression and legacy be?

Does this mean that fighting can never be a legitimate response? There may be instances where individuals, who are able consciously to make the choice for peace, choose nevertheless to fight. I find it hard to conceive of any circumstances where I could make that choice personally. However, it is an integral part of a loving response to others to respect the heartfelt choices they make.

We may fight for our homeland and yet it is only in our willingness not to fight that we may open to realise our original nature and experience coming home. Such is the paradox and irony of war. What we take by force is taken from us. What we lose is the chance to discover our deeper original self and to learn how to love from the inside out.

In our blindness, we may fight and sacrifice our life. And in our wakefulness, we can surrender the need to fight and truly learn how to live.

If we can soothe and learn how to step beyond our hunger and greed for more, we will experience the love, freedom and peace for which we have fought and outwardly searched.

Something
in our living dies
and in our dying lives.

Living our Dying

Why did I find it so very difficult to stay in the room when my dearest friend was so close to death? Maybe we are unable to face in others that which we deny in ourselves. I look back often to this time and wish that I had more willingly sought to befriend death a little earlier.

We forget that dying is natural. Is this because our great fear and the finality of death threatens our imagined omnipotence, so that we push away and banish every thought of death from life? This makes dying seem unnatural.

Strangely, I wonder if life without a conscious awareness of death can ever be wholly fulfilling. And so in fearing death as the ultimate unknown, we blindly throw away the only key which can unlock the secret of how to live life to the full.

Our challenge is to consider what meaning death might bring to our lives. But can we open to experience death and life more as a natural twin-ship and so engage more fully in this relationship, rather than reacting and seeking to sever it?

Our dying may offer a unique invitation to enter the vast unknown and maybe a vital chance to learn how to see beyond the need to know. Then might we come to know something of the vital mystery of creation itself?

Death may present us with the most profound paradox.

Our need to know with certainty closes the door upon our relationship with dying and the vital mystery of death. If we could resist the temptation to answer and know for sure, might we be able to enter into this vast unknown more willingly and there patiently discover, ever waiting, the answer for which we have searched all our lives?

If we can reconcile the drive to know and release our grip and control, will we discover that which calls to be known and is vital to our life? There, beyond our fears, in the quiet spaciousness of not having to know, might we discover the key to a fulfilled and meaningful life?

As we evade death, so we equally evade life. Might the intimacy of our relationship with death determine the degree to which we can intimately relate in our lives? Maybe there is profound value and meaning in bringing death to life and life to death.

Our living and dying is as natural to nature as her seasons. Can we therefore consider death to be less a full stop and more a comma in our unfolding story? At the heart of our every winter lies a dormant seed that forever dreams of spring.

What a paradox. If death, the place where we fear we will be most lost, is the only place where we are truly found. In dying and as we surrender, are we invited to discover a secret gift of an inner compass? This may be the only guide who can ever lead us home.

In surrendering to the inevitability of death we may therefore be given a key which paradoxically opens the door to the secret of living life fully.

Might dying be our only tutor to teach the vital art of surrender? Maybe the wise befriend this teacher and learn of this secret in life.

Might our dying teach us how to see beyond our search for certainty and the drive to know and so help us to remember and open to that which longs to be known – our emerging original self?

In realising the closer intimacy between our dying and living are we invited to discover the other within – the inner observer that is our vital partner? Might we, in borrowing the eyes of this other, become a witness to both our life and also possibly death? Can we perceive or conceive of that which may be deathless?

Could there be a vital source beyond the living which ever animates life? I wonder.

As we forgive our dream of omnipotence and can surrender our false eternity, then – and only then – might we glimpse the eternal? And as we surrender, perhaps we can reflect upon our often cruel and unnatural need to be perfect and instead relax in the freedom and comfort of knowing limitation.

Perfection, to which we may aspire, hides (but is never lost) behind the many veils of our imperfections. Let us lift each veil tenderly and with respect. Sight is born from seeing blindness. Only through seeing limitation can we open our eyes to that which is beyond.

In the practice of the art of surrender, in seeking to embrace mystery with confidence, we may meet with faith. This is a living paradox, for faith is a confidence in that which can never be certain or proven. Faith is an inner knowing: comfort and surety born from the knowledge of our inner experience which is ever a mystery and beyond any rational certainty.

Faith is never truly blind. Rather, it opens the eyes of the blind to see the mystery of who we truly are.

Faith is a gift that we are invited to discover. It cannot be given or taken: it is only to be discovered for ourselves. Faith holds hands with freedom in befriending the unknown by revealing that which longs to be known. It celebrates in discovering the creative mystery of not having to know.

The central paradox which death can guide us to appreciate or even resolve is that dying is the only teacher who can guide us how to live life fully. Only in surrendering and emptying ourselves of what we know can we fill with the experience of what longs to be known. Thus we remember that which inspires us to become the person we long to be. From what was once the dark unknown, a vital rose may blossom into our awareness, unveiling the secret of how to live our life and death without regret.

The creative mystery of dying and death teaches the art and practice of how, consciously, to let go. Through the insight and practice of surrender, we can discover we are already that for which we have endlessly searched. As we open to and become our original nature, we return home.

When all we have is taken – for everything we have and own will in time be taken – then, and only then, may we be given the greatest gift. We spend our lives looking for love. How strange and wonderful it would be at the end of our searching, when all is surrendered – even to our last breath – if then and there love finds us.

*Upon reflection
there is only
perfect imperfection.*

Concluding Reflections

I began composing this book when I became aware of my reaction of turning a blind eye and negating any sense of direct responsibility for a number of the crucial dilemmas of our modern times. War, for example, was not my problem, but theirs. I felt then that the reaction or response of one individual counted for little.

Today, through the development of this book and what has become a life-changing journey, my view has shifted profoundly. The conclusions I draw together, like the process of self-realisation, are a continuing discovery and revelation.

I have realised time and again that the self is my only original reference. This is the lens through which we learn to see and discover ourselves and the reality of the world around us, even though we commonly search for the answer elsewhere.

The self is not fixed or finite. Our vision changes to the same extent that we are able to open to discover original self. Irrespective of the point of our inner journey at which we have each arrived, we see the world as we are. I realise now that I can love, lead, inspire, relate to, understand and forgive others only to the same degree that I permit my self these experiences.

Though we commonly search outwardly for the answer, we learn how to see and relate from the inside out.

In turning away from our deeper original nature, we become blind to our potential and possibility. It is a sobering realisation that with this blindness we create the antithesis of that for which we long, without a sense of responsibility, or an appreciation of how we may unconsciously impact ourselves, others, culture and nature.

Denial of what we fear, be this the unknown mystery or potency of our original nature, divides the self. In the act of denial, we split and banish unwanted aspects of our self to the very edge of our consciousness and beyond. This fragments our vision and inner harmony. Do we, through this inner division, blindly manifest that which we most fear – a growing sense of loneliness, alienation and impotence? Can we learn to accept and lovingly embrace the person who seeks high ideals and yet blindly creates the very antithesis?

Denial not only divides, it also profoundly disorientates – we turn ourselves inside out. As a result, we are compelled to search outwardly for that one thing or something more that will satisfy and complete us; yet we forget to look within. Although on the surface, life's journey appears to be an outward search, I see now that we search for that which we already are and have. The outer trophy we seek is maybe more an inner destiny. In our outward drive to find the answer, we turn away from, and lose touch with, our deeper emerging self. The feeling that something is profoundly missing from our lives may be less a need to search and more a longing to remember the vital something more.

How quickly we forget to remember.

That we are partially sighted and sleeping are important and often forgotten aspects of our humanity. We are each invited to accept this insight with humility together with the chance to awaken and learn how to expand our vision. A key question for each of us is: in whom do we place our trust to lead, judge and to see clearly?

In composing this work, I realise that I am awakened more fully from my own sleeping by the presence of nature and also those rare individuals who – as a result of their own inner journey – can offer love, compassion and quality of attention without judgement or condition.

Both nature and these rare individuals inspire a memory of a forgotten intimate relationship.

Often I am drawn to photograph the empty chair in natural settings. Though this subject is outside, I am inspired to remember something or someone other within. Symbolically, the empty chair in nature also represents an inner experience. This is the place from which I am able to remember my deeper original nature. Here, beyond the urgency to do, I can at last be my self. From this inner viewpoint, I am able to see how I blindly react. In seeing my blindness, my vision naturally expands beyond its own limitation. Paradoxically, if I accept my limitation and impotence, I am reminded of a vital choice. This opens a new window through which we can look in, to discover our deeper original nature and self, and out, to see the world afresh.

This opens a new window
through which we can look in, to discover our original nature and self,
and out, to see the world afresh.

*The empty chair offers an open invitation
to meet and converse with the stranger within
who I seem to know as intimately as my self.*

The empty chair offers an open invitation to meet and converse with the stranger within who I seem to know as intimately as my self.

Our ability to move from an outward search to an inward journey may hinge upon our capacity to surrender our need to search and take our place upon the empty chair within. Our rational thinking may see surrender superficially as losing and giving up. Surrender is, however, the art and practice of willingly letting go of what we have or seek, in order to remember that which is vital to our life. In surrendering, we empty and forget, so that we can fill with and remember the memory of that which ever motivates our becoming.

Do we face the ultimate act of surrender in our dying and at the point of death as an invitation to embrace and remember our vital mystery and otherness? In living with the realisation that we are dying, we bring surrender to life. It is only in the acceptance of our dying that we learn the secret of how to live life in all its fullness. In this way, do we transform loss into a vital gain?

The experience of the empty chair invites the discovery of both self and inner other. Though outwardly life seems to be a search for the single absolute answer, inwardly, as we open to discover our deeper original nature, we are met by a dynamic contradiction and paradox.

I have come to realise in composing this book that the possible resolution of crucial dilemmas in our modern world may depend upon our capacity to value and accept dilemma and paradox as the natural expression of our deeper original nature. In meeting with and accepting the dilemma of the self, we are guided and invited to see the reality of the world around us quite differently.

In this way, our inner journey offers the rare chance for us to know difference – differently.

Outwardly, in our first meeting with difference, we experience its polarity. An immediate impulse and the pull of our rational thinking is to divide difference in judging this to be right or that to be wrong. However, in remembering our deeper nature and paradox, we are invited to discover an inner capacity to relate more intimately. Without the need to rationalise or solve, what emerges is a new possibility for a deeper exploration and contemplation of our dilemmas. No longer tempted to analyse, we can instead take time to question our need to answer – entering deeper into the heart of the dilemma to formulate and ask the vital questions.

The natural paradox of our deeper nature can teach us how to hold gently both right and wrong, whilst also inviting the possibility of the something more to emerge. Might the resolution of our dilemmas depend more on our ability and capacity to accept contradiction as natural and in this realisation be more able to ask the vital question rather than to rationalise, judge or answer?

Though denial may split and divide us from our deeper nature, we are naturally deeply relational beings.

As we open to discover the innate contradiction of our deeper nature and how we can blindly divide, we are gifted with a growing capacity to embrace and can therefore enter into a new, more intimate and loving relationship with conflict and dilemma.

In our ability to contemplate conflict deeply, we may become more aware of previously hidden harmonies and new possibilities of communion. In this way, we are able to embrace more fully the polarity of difference, conflict and dilemma with renewed hope and possibility of resolution.

As we discover our original nature, we find a depth and a natural contradiction to our lives that has its own dynamic vitality and soulfulness. In accepting paradox, a sense of urgency is lulled by the comfort of not needing to know or find the answer. We can now experience the deep mystery of self. In willingly entering into this mystery, we transform a fear of the unknown into a vital curiosity. Beyond this fear, what we may begin to see instead is a dynamic and creative paradox. From this inner viewpoint, what once secured my impotence now becomes my motivation and new found freedom.

In meeting with our original nature, we permit ourselves to accept all that is strange and unfamiliar as an innate expression of our originality.

As I accept my limitations, I unveil and allow a deeper compassion, love, peace, joy and freedom to emerge. Here, within the loving arms of paradox, head finds heart and we can conceive and imagine the gentleness needed to soothe that which hungers within. We find the tenderness and compassion to see and face our fragility more as an inner strength.

As I realise my deeper original nature, I am invited to remember the intimacy of my original relationship with nature. We are not outside of nature, but know nature intimately and inside out. Nature asks that we accept its natural rhythms and cycles as vital aspects of our soulfulness and deeper humanity. Nature ever inspires our journey to realise our original nature and in our willingness to accept and take this natural remedy, we and society can heal.

Though we may be tempted to turn away from the challenge to face and contemplate contradiction and dilemma, it is a natural expression of our deeper nature. In discovering the dynamic paradox and mystery of original self, we are invited to expand our capacity not only to see and sense, but also to relate and resolve. In this realisation, we can move from the belief that we exist only as part that searches to become whole and complete, to realise that we are both a part from, and a part of, that which is already whole and complete.

Might our outward search for a partner, important as it is, be only an echo of the inner experience of that which is one, unbroken and complete which we are invited to discover? In the realisation of the paradox of our partial oneness, the boundaries of self and other dissolve. We open instead to experience both an individual and collective awareness which seems to have intention. Our separateness and division is completed by an experience of the oneness of our original relationship.

*As we open to discover original self, the faculties of conscience and
imagination blossom within.*

In this discovery and vital reorientation, the divisions of inside and out, individual and collective and even past and future seem to dissolve into the immediacy and prospect of the present moment. This experience of a relatedness of all things mirrors that of our original nature and reality. Our senses can now expand and deepen with this awareness to receive new insights, a deepening intuition and moments of illumination.

New inner faculties emerge that can expand and deepen our capacity to see and sense and to conceive and create.

As we open to discover original self, the faculties of conscience and imagination blossom within. Rather than searching outwardly for the answer, an inner presence and compassionate reference emerges to guide us from within. This guide offers an inner compass to which we can orientate and affirm the chosen direction of our lives. Paradoxically, as we are invited to accept the depth, breadth and magnitude of our natural tide and cycle, we discover a deeper sense of resilience.

The power and potency of the original self becomes the source and energy of our intention that motivates our choices and how we respond. The energy of our intention is a measure of the degree to which we can surrender to the will that inspires our becoming. This is the power to listen deeply and to evolve and co-create.

Our intention is a loving desire that longs to take form.

Our imagination is an inner alchemist that can change our base metal into gold by transforming our thoughts from intention into reality. This vital desire flows towards its own natural conclusion in the same way that a river finds the sea. The promise of original self is of self-fulfilment through self-acceptance. To be in service of this longing is our second nature. As we open to the gift of acceptance from experiencing our deeper nature, so we can also naturally inspire others to discover their own.

As we align with that which is vital to our life, we free our imagination to conceive of all that we long for in our lives and society. It is important to recognise that the harmony and peace which we may desire has first to be conceived and experienced by someone. The person I aspire to be and become, and the society in which I would love to live, I am – and we are – invited to conceive from within.

As we discover our original nature, are we being invited to see how we unconsciously react and to expand our consciousness to embrace that which is one and unbroken – to become the artists who are inspired to give this new, unfamiliar and expanded awareness form and novel expression. We expand as we remember the artist within: that is, our creative originality.

Might our individual and collective growth relate to the degree to which the inner faculties of a wise and compassionate conscience and a free imagination emerge to guide and shape how we respond? Only in this way can we free ourselves from the unconscious grip to participate consciously in the process of becoming.

*Might love be the expression of original self
and the remembering of our original capacity to relate?*

I felt at the beginning of this journey that to make a difference of one I may need to do something more: find an answer or solution. My conclusion is much more subtle. It is only in my willingness to surrender the need to search that I can remember and return to the discovery of my deeper nature. I see now that the answer lies more in my capacity to accept my original nature, whether I am sleeping or awakening, becoming or returning. Only when I can fully embrace this contradiction and accept the paradox of my deeper self do I realise the choice to respond. In the discovery of original self, I am invited to learn how to love my soulfulness in all its strange and vital originality and how to embrace lovingly otherness – and all others.

In taking this inner journey, I have transformed fear into faith. For my self, faith is an emerging and deepening capacity to trust in that which is unknown and unknowable and yet is vital and innate to my humanity. With faith, I am given the rare chance to embrace lovingly the stranger within as my self. In the acceptance of this vital paradox, I can learn to bear equally my pain and joy, sorrow and happiness and maybe all that is dark and light without fear or a need to reject – to accept this more as a vital and creative otherness.

As we discover our deeper nature, do we remember and can experience the emotions we have denied, including both love and fear? Are we therefore invited, without the need to solve or answer, to bear our humanity and contemplate our responsibility and reason for being? Might this response fulfil our name sake as human beings? I wonder....

As we realise our capacity and choice to surrender our needs – to take, to have, to find, to own, to know and to fight – might we then be met by love and peace?

Only in the discovery of that which is changeless are we immeasurably changed.

Might love be the expression of original self and the remembering of our original capacity to relate? Might love be both our destiny and origin? Love has no other need than to fulfil its own intention – to be and become. Love is the capacity to accept the unfamiliar stranger without condition or judgement. Through love we may expand our sensitivity to embrace self and other, even culture and nature. Love seeks no power, for love is the innate source of power that we receive and the secret potency and gift of original self.

Maybe the peace makers are at peace and the lovers of life are in love from the inside out.

Might all this – and more – be and become the contribution and legacy of a difference of one.

Only in the discovery of that which is changeless
are we immeasurably changed.